Author: Kaido Väinamäe

ISBN HARDBACK: 978-1-80560-177-7

ISBN PAPERBACK: 978-1-80560-642-0

## Eternal Threads

In weaving light, we find our way,
Threads of gold, through night and day.
Binding dreams, with every sigh,
Hearts entwined, as stars drift by.

Through shadows cast, our colors blend,
A tapestry that has no end.
Whispers soft, that time can't sever,
Together strong, we are forever.

## Boundless Harmony

In melodies that softly soar,
A rhythm found, we yearn for more.
Notes entwined in sweet refrain,
Together, weathering joy and pain.

Hand in hand, we face the dawn,
With every step, we are reborn.
In nature's song, our spirits rise,
Boundless love, beneath the skies.

## Boundless Echoes of Togetherness

In the quiet of the night, we stand,
Hearts entwined like a woven strand.
Laughter dancing in the air,
Two souls merging, beyond compare.

Whispers carried by the breeze,
A symphony that puts us at ease.
With every heartbeat, our spirits sing,
In unity, we find our wings.

Moments shared beneath the moon,
Time melts away, a sweet cocoon.
Hands entwined, unfurling tight,
Together we blaze, a radiant light.

Through storms that challenge and sway,
We navigate our own bright way.
In the tapestry of life we weave,
Boundless echoes, we believe.

In the dawn's embrace, we rise,
Chasing dreams that touch the skies.
Together, we're forever strong,
In this bond where we belong.

## Synergy of Stars

In the canvas of a velvet night,
Stars align in glorious sight.
Each twinkle tells a tale of fate,
A cosmic dance we celebrate.

Gravity pulls, yet we soar,
In the heartbeat of the evermore.
Each dream ignited, bright and true,
In the silence, it's me and you.

Whispers of the universe call,
A serenade that binds us all.
In this galaxy, we play our part,
Together, we craft a radiant art.

As constellations paint the sky,
Our spirits merge, reaching high.
In the synergy, we find our place,
Stars embracing in endless grace.

Time may fade, yet we will shine,
In every moment, love is divine.
Through the cosmos, side by side,
In this journey, we abide.

## The Unbreakable Bonds

In the fabric where our stories blend,
Through trials faced, hand in hand we mend.
Life's tempests may batter and fight,
Yet, together, we find the light.

Threads of laughter, woven tight,
Holding fast through the darkest night.
Each shared glance, an honest truth,
Igniting the fire of our youth.

In the maze of life, we wander free,
Tethered by heartstrings, you and me.
Our roots intertwined, a steady ground,
In the silence, love's echoes sound.

With every challenge, we will rise,
Trusting the bond we hold so wise.
Against the odds, we stand so tall,
In unbreakable bonds, we never fall.

As seasons change and rivers flow,
In this connection, we will grow.
Through every chapter, near or far,
Together, always, our guiding star.

# Celestial Embrace

Under the blanket of the endless night,
We find solace in the soft moonlight.
In the stillness, our hearts align,
In a celestial embrace, so divine.

The cosmos hums a lullaby sweet,
With every heartbeat, our souls meet.
Stars wink gently, sharing their glow,
In the universe, love starts to grow.

Galaxies swirl, a vivid array,
Together we journey, come what may.
In this expanse, we carve our name,
In a dance of light, never the same.

As comets streak across the sky,
We dare to dream, to soar, to fly.
In celestial arms, we intertwine,
Forever in rhythm, your heart with mine.

With every sunrise, a brand new chance,
In this embrace, we find our dance.
Together as one, we will chase,
The timeless love in our celestial space.

# Unity in Motion

In the heart, a rhythm beats,
As every soul in silence greets.
Together we rise, hand in hand,
In this dance, we take a stand.

With whispers soft, we share our dreams,
Flowing like rivers, pure and keen.
Each heartbeat echoes, strong and true,
Bound by the ties that link me and you.

In the twilight, shadows blend,
We weave a tapestry, no end.
Side by side, our spirits soar,
Finding strength in what we explore.

The sound of laughter fills the air,
Every moment, a gift we share.
Unity forms the gentle thread,
In motion, our stories spread.

Together we paint the sky at dawn,
With hues of hope, the dark is gone.
In unity, we find our way,
Forever in motion, come what may.

# The Infinity of Us

In every glance, a spark ignites,
A cosmic dance of radiant lights.
Infinite moments woven tight,
In the silence, we take flight.

Through the chaos, we find the calm,
In our embrace, the world feels warm.
Stars align, our paths entwined,
In the depths, our souls unwind.

Beyond the limits of time and space,
Together we navigate every place.
In the echoes, our hearts conjoin,
An endless loop, a sacred coin.

With every heartbeat, love expands,
An infinite journey, hand in hand.
Beyond measure, our spirits trust,
In the infinity, it's always us.

Through every storm, we hold our ground,
In the silence, our truth is found.
With every breath, we'll rise anew,
In this boundless love, me and you.

## Unfolding Together

In the garden, seeds of hope,
We plant our dreams and learn to cope.
Each petal opens, revealing grace,
A gentle smile upon our face.

With every step, the path grows clear,
In our journey, we shed the fear.
Together we rise through every tear,
Finding beauty in what is dear.

Layers peel back, revealing light,
As shadows dance, we ignite.
An unfolding tale of love and trust,
In unity, it's always just.

The world around us gleams so bright,
In every corner, we find the light.
Hand in hand, we walk this way,
Unfolding together every day.

With arms wide open, we embrace,
The journey we share, time can't erase.
In the tapestry of life we weave,
Unfolding together, we believe.

# Celestial Dance

Underneath the starry skies,
We twirl, lost in each other's eyes.
The moonlight whispers, soft and low,
In this celestial dance, we flow.

Every heartbeat a note, sublime,
In this universe, we carve our rhyme.
With every turn, our spirits leap,
In the cosmos, our secrets keep.

Galaxies spin, tracing our dreams,
In the silence, our laughter beams.
Eclipsing doubts, we shine so bright,
In this dance, we own the night.

Stars align to guide our way,
Through the darkness, we find our play.
In this rhythm, we've made our stand,
Bound together, hand in hand.

With every twinkle, a promise grows,
In endless skies, our love bestows.
As time flows, we will waltz renewed,
In this celestial dance, we're imbued.

# The Fabric of Us

In every weave, a story laid,
Threads of laughter, unafraid.
Colors bright, a vibrant dance,
In this tapestry, we enhance.

Moments stitched with care and grace,
Endless patterns we embrace.
Through the storms, our fibers hold,
Each strand a memory, bold.

Love and loss, they intertwine,
In this fabric, hearts align.
Woven tight, through thick and thin,
Together we rise, together we win.

In shadows cast, we find the light,
Illuminate the darkest night.
Every stitch, a promise made,
In the fabric, never fade.

A tapestry that spans all time,
In every thread, a silent rhyme.
Forever sewn, our bond so true,
In the fabric, me and you.

## Celestial Convergence

Stars align in night's embrace,
Cosmic dance, a timeless trace.
Galaxies swirl, in grand display,
Infinite wonders lead the way.

Planets whisper, secrets old,
Stories of the brave and bold.
In the silence of the void,
A symphony of peace enjoyed.

Comets streak across the sky,
Carving paths where dreams may lie.
Constellations spark the mind,
In this vastness, love we find.

Eclipses linger, shadows fall,
In the wonder, we hear the call.
Unity in the cosmic sea,
Together in our destiny.

In this dance, we find our place,
Through the vastness, we chase grace.
Bound by love's celestial tune,
In convergence, we become the moon.

# Unbroken Circles

Life's a loop, a constant spin,
In every loss, we may begin.
Seasons change, yet still they stay,
In our hearts, they'll find a way.

With every end, a brand new start,
Cycles flow, a work of art.
In the echoes, voices call,
Unbroken circles, we'll not fall.

Through the trials, we will grow,
In every high, you'll find a low.
Bound together, hand in hand,
In this circle, we will stand.

Tender moments intertwine,
In the rhythm, we align.
Love's embrace, a sacred pact,
In the circle, that's a fact.

Time may bend, but it won't sway,
In this dance, we find our way.
Unbroken bonds, forever near,
In love's circle, we persevere.

# Threads of Forever

Each thread we weave, a tale unfolds,
In colors rich, stories told.
Lifetimes stitched in patterns bright,
In every weave, a glimpse of light.

Silken strands, a bond so tight,
Through darkest days and endless night.
In every knot, the love we share,
A tapestry beyond compare.

Forever spans in every hue,
In threads of gold, me and you.
The needle pulls, the moments flow,
In this fabric, love will grow.

From whispered dreams to shouts of glee,
Each fiber holds our history.
Through the years, as seasons blend,
In threads of forever, we transcend.

Let storms come, let shadows fall,
In our weaving, we stand tall.
For every thread that binds us strong,
In love's embrace, we all belong.

## Unified Whispers

In shadows cast, our voices blend,
A gentle hum, the heart's extend.
Together we're a quiet force,
In unity, we find our course.

Each echo soft, yet bold and clear,
Resounding truths that draw us near.
In whispered dreams, we claim our space,
Unified, we find our grace.

With every challenge that we face,
We share the load, we share the pace.
A tapestry of souls entwined,
In whispers, strength is redefined.

Through nights of doubt and days of light,
Our bond transforms, igniting might.
The strength of many, one heart beat,
Unified, we rise, complete.

Beyond the noise, we seek the calm,
In tender tones, we craft our balm.
In union's song, our spirits soar,
Together, we are evermore.

# Symphony of Being

In vibrant hues, we paint our lives,
Each note a story, where love thrives.
Together, we compose the tune,
A symphony that makes us bloom.

With every heartbeat, every sigh,
Harmony calls, we reach the sky.
In contrasts bold, we find the blend,
In every note, our voices mend.

The rhythm pulses, strong and true,
In every chord, a piece of you.
Through peaks and valleys, we will play,
A symphony that leads the way.

In softest whispers or loudest cries,
We find our strength, no need for lies.
Each moment shared, a precious thread,
In this grand song, our spirits spread.

Together, we embrace the sound,
In pure connection, we are found.
A melody of hearts laid bare,
In symphony, we find our care.

# Tides of Togetherness

The ocean's breath, a rhythmic dance,
In waves, a spirit's sweet romance.
As tides arise, we join the flow,
Together, we will let it show.

Each ebb and tide, a pull and push,
In harmony, we feel the rush.
Through every surge, we find our place,
In togetherness, there's boundless grace.

With every ripple, trust will grow,
In seas of love, we learn, we know.
With open hearts, we voyage far,
In unity, we reach for stars.

The sun may set, the moon will rise,
Yet in each other, truth's disguise.
Through depths unknown, we navigate,
In tides of love, we celebrate.

With currents strong, we face the fight,
Together, we embrace the night.
In every wave, a song of us,
In tides of togetherness, we trust.

# The Power of We

In whispered dreams, our hopes align,
Together, we ignite and shine.
Each heartbeat echoes 'you and me',
In shared intent, we find the key.

The strength of many fuels the flame,
In unity, we claim our name.
Hand in hand, we face the storm,
In every trial, we keep warm.

With voices loud, we challenge fate,
Through shared resolve, we navigate.
In every struggle, side by side,
Together, we rise, our hearts our guide.

With arms outstretched, we lift each other,
In this embrace, we find our mother.
The world may change, but one thing's true,
In power of we, we can renew.

Our stories weave a vibrant thread,
In laughter shared, in tears we've shed.
For every dream and every plea,
In love's embrace lies the power of we.

## Boundless Interconnection

In every breath, we share the air,
Threads of life weave everywhere.
Our spirits dance, a cosmic art,
In every soul, we find a part.

Mountains tall and oceans wide,
In each heartbeat, we confide.
Nature's pulse, a gentle tune,
Underneath the same bright moon.

Every smile, a bridge we span,
In laughter, we create a plan.
Hands together, strong we stand,
In this waltz, we hold the land.

Time unveils our destiny,
In shared dreams, we roam free.
Boundless paths that intertwine,
In the end, it's yours and mine.

Each story told, a thread revealed,
Within our hearts, the truth sealed.
Together we sing life's refrain,
In this bond, no one in vain.

# The Chorus of Existence

Listen closely, hear the call,
In every whisper, we stand tall.
Harmony dances in the breeze,
Nature sings, it aims to please.

With every step, a rhythm flows,
United in the highs and lows.
Each heartbeat, a note in the air,
Together we rise, lift, and share.

Voices join in vibrant hues,
Songs of life in varied views.
The essence of joy intertwines,
In every spirit, love aligns.

Echoes of laughter, tears that spill,
In moments shared, we find our will.
A symphony composed of dreams,
Together we paint, or so it seems.

Through the storms and brightest skies,
In this chorus, compassion lies.
We sing of hope, of life, of love,
A reminder we're guided from above.

# Waves of Togetherness

Rising tides, a gentle wave,
Together we learn, together brave.
In every ebb, a bond we find,
An ocean deep, two hearts aligned.

Rippling laughter, shared delight,
In quiet moments, we ignite.
Bridging gaps, we drift as one,
In the twilight, our spirits run.

Every wave a story told,
In the current, we break the mold.
Shores that touch where waters meet,
Together, our journey is complete.

As the tide pulls us, we flow,
In the stillness, our love will grow.
Hand in hand, we face the night,
In the waves, we find our light.

Each crest and trough, a memory made,
In the depths, our fears will fade.
Waves of hope crash on the sand,
Together we rise, forever stand.

# Resonating Together

In each sound, a truth we find,
Resonating, our hearts aligned.
A symphony of voices strong,
In each note, we all belong.

Echoes carry through the air,
Vibrations whisper that we care.
United we stand, a vibrant sound,
In this chorus, love is found.

Melodies weave, stories shared,
In the silence, we are bared.
Each heartbeat a rhythm that plays,
Connected in so many ways.

In harmony, we rise and fall,
Cascading notes, we hear the call.
Together we dance, together we sing,
In this moment, we are everything.

When the world feels loud and bright,
In you and me, we find our light.
Resonating, strong and clear,
Together we conquer every fear.

# Unity in Diversity

In colors bright we find our kin,
A tapestry where all begin.
Each thread unique, a story told,
Together we weave, a blend of bold.

Voices rise in harmonious song,
In differences, we all belong.
Hands joined as one, we face the day,
In unity's light, we find our way.

Through laughter's echo and tears shared,
The strength is found, we feel prepared.
Celebrate all, in heart and mind,
In the dance of life, true peace we find.

Step forward with pride, no fear to show,
With open hearts, let kindness grow.
Together we'll stand, embrace the fight,
For in our union, we ignite the light.

So here we stand, a vibrant group,
In this vast world, we make our loop.
Different yet one, we stake our claim,
In unity's fire, we fan the flame.

# The Living Circle

In nature's arms, life finds its way,
A circle formed in night and day.
From seed to bloom, the journey flows,
In gentle whispers, this life bestows.

The sun will rise, the moon will gleam,
In every heart, a vital dream.
Seasons change, yet love remains,
In every pulse, the cycle gains.

Down rivers we drift, on winds we glide,
Each twist and turn, we trust the tide.
The earth spins forth, a dance divine,
In every soul, our paths align.

From mountain high to ocean's flow,
A bond unbroken, forever grow.
In unity's dance, we find our role,
Together as one, we are whole.

The living circle, a sacred thread,
Connects all hearts, both near and spread.
In every breath, a shared embrace,
Life's endless rhythm, in time and space.

# Beyond the Boundaries

In distant lands where dreams take flight,
We reach for stars beyond our sight.
With hearts ablaze, we break the walls,
In whispered hopes, adventure calls.

Mountains high and oceans wide,
Our spirits soar, we'll not abide.
For journey's end is not in sight,
In every step, we find the light.

Courage fuels our brave pursuit,
Through every trial, our roots take root.
With open minds, we cross the line,
In shared experience, we intertwine.

Beyond the borders, boundaries blur,
In every soul, the dreams concur.
In the tapestry of life, we weave,
A common thread, together believe.

So cast aside all fear and doubt,
Embrace the world that calls us out.
For in our voyage, we shall find,
Unity born from hearts entwined.

## Unfolding the Evermore

Each moment comes, a gift to share,
In dreams we weave, our hopes laid bare.
The future calls, a canvas wide,
In every heartbeat, love and pride.

Through time's embrace, we learn to grow,
In every challenge, strength will flow.
With open arms, we greet the dawn,
In this unfolding, we are reborn.

Beyond the past, we cast aside,
The burdens carried, the waves of tide.
In every breath, a chance to start,
A journey deep within the heart.

As seasons turn, the world transforms,
In every tempest, new light warms.
With eyes wide open, we explore,
In life's embrace, we seek much more.

So let us dance in present grace,
As time unfolds its endless space.
With each new step, we'll forge the way,
For in the evermore, we'll find our stay.

## Inextricable Threads

In the loom of life we weave,
Threads of joy, threads of grief.
Patterns intertwine and twist,
In every moment, we exist.

Silent whispers, tales unfold,
Stories of the young and old.
Every stitch a memory,
Binding us in harmony.

Colors vibrant, shades of grey,
Each decision, choice we weigh.
Through the fabric, pain and light,
Create the tapestry of night.

Entwined in love and sorrow,
Hope we craft for tomorrow.
Holding tight, we never sever,
Inextricable threads forever.

## The Dance of Wholeness

Beneath the stars, we find our feet,
In the rhythm of life's heartbeat.
Every step a sacred chance,
We twirl together in this dance.

Whispers breeze through branches high,
Lifting spirits, making us fly.
Harmony in every move,
In this unity, we groove.

Voices rise, a chorus strong,
In our hearts, where we belong.
With every touch, we share the grace,
In this waltz, we find our place.

Spinning lightly, joy abounds,
In this space, love surrounds.
In the dance of wholeness, we see,
Each beat, a vibrant melody.

# Celestial Kin

Under the vast and twinkling skies,
We share the dreams that never die.
Stars align, we find our way,
In celestial warmth, we lay.

Cosmic bonds, unbroken ties,
Connected hearts in starlit highs.
Through the darkness, light will shine,
Guiding us, our souls entwined.

Galaxies dance in silent grace,
Each heartbeat finds its rightful place.
Infinite realms we are a part,
Celestial kin, hand in heart.

In every spark, a story gleams,
Carried on the wings of dreams.
Together we soar, forever free,
In cosmic love, eternally.

## Unison in Diversity

In the garden, colors bloom,
Each petal sings, dispels the gloom.
Unity in differences,
A symphony of experiences.

Voices rise, a joyful throng,
Every tone, every song.
Together we forge a brand new path,
In the light of love, we laugh.

Rich and rare, the shades we bring,
Hope and courage, in us, cling.
Hand in hand, we walk this way,
Diverse and bright, we choose to stay.

Every background, a thread of gold,
Weaving stories yet untold.
In unison, we rise to see,
The beauty found in you and me.

# The Symphony of Together

In harmony we find our song,
As hearts unite, we all belong.
Each note a whisper, soft and clear,
Together, we cast away all fear.

With hands entwined, we dance in time,
A chorus born of every climb.
United voices, strong and true,
In every rhythm, there's me and you.

Moments woven, threads so bright,
In twilight's glow, we share the light.
With every heartbeat, joys resound,
In this symphony, love is found.

Through trials faced and laughter shared,
In every silence, we have dared.
A melody of trust we weave,
In one another, we believe.

So let our voices rise and swell,
In this grand tale, we weave our spell.
Forever together, we'll remain,
In the symphony of love, our gain.

## Interlaced Journeys

Two paths that twist and gently turn,
With every step, we learn and yearn.
Through valleys deep and mountains high,
Together, we reach for the sky.

In every stumble, hands reach out,
With faith ignited, there's no doubt.
From distant places, we emerge,
In shared adventure, hearts converge.

The stories told beneath the stars,
Each moment cherished, never far.
As shadows fade and dawn appears,
We hold each other through our fears.

In laughter's echo, sorrow too,
The journey shared is always true.
Side by side, we brave the tide,
In interlaced journeys, we abide.

With every mile, a bond we hold,
A treasure deep, more rare than gold.
Our spirits rise as we roam free,
In these intertwined paths, we'll be.

## The Confluence of Lives

Where rivers meet and hearts collide,
In every moment, love's our guide.
With each connection, stories blend,
In the confluence, we transcend.

From different shores, we all arrive,
In unity, we come alive.
Each twist and turn, a chance to grow,
In shared experiences, we glow.

Through laughter's spark and tearful streams,
We build our castles made of dreams.
In vibrant hues, our lives entwined,
A tapestry of hearts combined.

With every breath, our spirits soar,
In this embrace, we yearn for more.
Together we face both joy and strife,
In the confluence of our lives.

A river's flow, a gentle guide,
With open hearts, we'll turn the tide.
In every heartbeat, love does thrive,
In our confluence, we are alive.

# Everlasting Bonds

In every glance, a story told,
Through years we've shared, a love of gold.
With laughter rippling through our days,
In every moment, our hearts blaze.

As seasons change, our roots run deep,
In every promise, memories keep.
Through trials faced and joys embraced,
In every touch, our essence traced.

Together we rise, together we stand,
Through ebb and flow, hand in hand.
In whispered dreams, we find our right,
In everlasting bonds, pure light.

With every sunset that paints the sky,
We gather close as time slips by.
With every heartbeat, strong and free,
Our love's the anchor, you and me.

So let the world around us sway,
In the heart's embrace, we'll find our way.
Forever cherished, never gone,
In this dance of life, we carry on.

## Boundless Embrace

In the quiet of twilight's glow,
Hearts entwined, a gentle flow,
Whispers dance on evening air,
Love's embrace, beyond compare.

Stars awaken in the night,
Promises whisper, pure delight,
Together woven, strong and bold,
A tale of love, forever told.

Through valleys deep and mountains high,
We chase the dreams, we learn to fly,
Hand in hand, we face the storms,
In your warmth, my spirit warms.

Every moment, a sacred thread,
Every glance spun, softly spread,
Boundless love in every gaze,
In your heart, I find my place.

As seasons change, our roots grow deep,
In this bond, our secrets keep,
Forever cherished, we will stay,
In this boundless embrace, come what may.

# Alchemy of Souls

In the furnace of passion, we ignite,
Two souls merging, pure and bright,
Fires burn with ancient flame,
Transforming hearts, we are not the same.

Waves of magic, ebb and flow,
In this dance, we learn and grow,
Threads of fate, we intertwine,
An alchemy divine, so fine.

With every touch, we spark the night,
Spirit whispers, pure delight,
In the shadows, secrets roam,
In your heart, I find my home.

Through trials faced, we rise anew,
Together strong, in all we do,
A potion brewed from joy and pain,
Love's alchemy, our hearts remain.

Through time and space, we journey far,
Guided always by our star,
In the crucible, we are whole,
An endless dance, the alchemy of soul.

## Tides of Connection

Beneath the moon, the waters sway,
Pulling hearts in a gentle play,
Waves of laughter, whispers soft,
Tides of connection, lifting oft.

In the currents, we find our way,
Through storms and calm, we choose to stay,
Hands entwined, we face the sea,
In your eyes, I am set free.

With every ripple, stories weave,
Songs of love, we both believe,
Shorelines shift, yet we remain,
In depths of trust, there's no more pain.

Riding waves of joy and sorrow,
In each tide, we find tomorrow,
Connected souls, forever near,
In this ocean, love is clear.

The horizon calls, adventures bright,
In unity, we hold the light,
As tides will ebb, and flow will see,
Together strong, forever free.

# The Connected Soul

In silence shared, our spirits know,
Paths of light where love will grow,
Hearts aligned in cosmic dance,
Two souls intertwine, a fateful chance.

With gentle words, we build a bridge,
Through whispered dreams, we leap the ridge,
Moments treasured, deeply felt,
In every heartbeat, love is dealt.

The universe hums a timeless tune,
Stars align beneath the moon,
Echoes of laughter, tears that flow,
In this connection, we learn and grow.

Through trials faced, together we stand,
Crafting futures, hand in hand,
In this bond, no fear shall take,
For our connected souls awake.

As journeys unfold, we'll navigate,
With every step, we celebrate,
In the tapestry of life, we find,
The beauty of love, perfectly aligned.

## Shared Dreams

In twilight's glow, we find our place,
With whispers soft, we share a space.
A world of hopes, woven so fine,
Together we chase, what's yours and mine.

With every thought, a thread we spin,
In silent vows, our hearts begin.
Through starry nights, our visions blend,
In dreams we soar, around the bend.

Across the sky, our wishes fly,
In sacred moments, just you and I.
Each heartbeat echoes, a gentle song,
In shared dreams, we both belong.

With morning light, the shadows fade,
In courage born, our fears are laid.
Together we'll rise, through dusk and dawn,
In the tapestry of dreams, love is drawn.

So hand in hand, we'll brave the storms,
In every shape, our bond transforms.
For in this dance, we both have grown,
In shared dreams, we are never alone.

# A Universe of Wholeness

In whispers soft, the cosmos calls,
With stardust dreams, we break our falls.
A universe vast, where love ignites,
In every heartbeat, the darkness lights.

Beyond the stars, our spirits meet,
In cosmic flows, we feel complete.
Through galaxies wide, we chase the light,
In endless night, our souls take flight.

With every breath, the planets sway,
In harmony found, we choose to stay.
A dance of life, in rhythm pure,
In this wholeness, we feel secure.

From mountain peaks to ocean's floor,
In nature's arms, we seek for more.
With open hearts, we bridge the space,
In the universe, we leave our trace.

So let us roam, let us explore,
In unity bound, forevermore.
A mosaic bright, a radiant whole,
In this vast universe, we find our soul.

# The Heart's Convergence

In gentle beats, our hearts collide,
With tender pulses, we cannot hide.
A meeting place where spirits dance,
In every glance, we find our chance.

Through crowded streets and quiet nights,
In every word, our love ignites.
A tapestry of stories spun,
In the convergence, we become one.

With hands entwined, we leave our mark,
In every tear, we fuel the spark.
Through the chaos, a calm we find,
In heart's convergence, our souls aligned.

With every sigh, our journey flows,
In silent thoughts, affection grows.
With shared laughter, our burdens ease,
In this embrace, we're sure to please.

So let us bask in moments rare,
In heart's sweet song, our love laid bare.
Together we'll walk this winding road,
In convergence found, we share our load.

## Confluence of Hearts

In merging streams, our lives entwine,
With passion's pulse, your heart is mine.
A river flows where echoes gleam,
In timeless rhythm, we live the dream.

With every touch, new worlds unfold,
In whispered secrets, stories told.
Through sunlit paths and shadowed bends,
In confluence dear, our love transcends.

With gentle grace, we find our way,
In storms of life, together stay.
A union bright, two flames in one,
Through thick and thin, our journey's begun.

In laughter shared, we melt the pain,
Through trials faced, our hearts remain.
In harmony's song, our spirits soar,
In love's embrace, we seek for more.

So let the rivers merge and blend,
In every corner, around the bend.
For in this confluence, we embark,
With hearts as one, we light the dark.

# Interwoven Destinies

In shadows deep, our paths entwine,
A flicker here, a glimmer there.
With every choice, a thread we bind,
Together spinning fate's fine air.

In swirling winds, our stories merge,
Two hearts that dance on time's great loom.
Through trials faced, our spirits surge,
In woven dreams, we find our home.

Each twist and turn, a lesson learned,
In laughter shared, in silence known.
A tapestry of love we've earned,
Our destinies in colors flown.

Through storms we stand, in sun we glow,
With every step, our bond grows strong.
Interlaced like rivers flow,
In harmony, we sing our song.

So let us tread this path with grace,
In every heartbeat, echoes rhyme.
With open hands, we embrace space,
For interwoven souls, in time.

## Harmony in Duality

In shadows cast, the light will play,
Two sides of us, both bright and dark.
Together we find a gentle sway,
A melody where all can hark.

In every storm, the calm will find,
The balance held, we hold it dear.
Through whispered words, our hearts aligned,
In union, we dissolve all fear.

The sun and moon, they share the sky,
Together in their dance divine.
With every breath, we learn to fly,
As one, we weave our fated line.

In laughter's echo, tears will find,
Their place beside the joy we show.
In duality, our souls combined,
Creating peace, we both will grow.

So let us cherish every phase,
In every shift, a chance to see.
With open hearts, we walk this maze,
In harmony, just you and me.

# The Unfolding Weave

Threads of life, each moment spun,
In colors bright, the past we trace.
With every breath, new tales begun,
An endless dance of time and space.

In gentle hands, the fiber flows,
We craft our fate with every thread.
Each knot a lesson that we chose,
In woven patterns, lives are led.

As seasons change, the tapestry,
Unfolds in beauty, rich and bold.
With every stitch, a memory,
In textures warm, our stories told.

Through laughter shared and sorrows paid,
This fabric holds our hopes and dreams.
The love we give, the joy we made,
In every line, our spirit beams.

So let us spin with hearts alive,
Creating more than what we see.
In vibrant hues, we shall arrive,
In the unfolding weave, we're free.

## Chorus of the Cosmos

In night's embrace, the stars will sing,
A chorus vast, of light and sound.
Each twinkle tells what time will bring,
A cosmic dance, where dreams are found.

Galaxies spin, the planets glide,
Together, in this boundless sea.
In every note, the heavens guide,
A melody of you and me.

From ancient myths, the tales take flight,
In every heart, a dream ignites.
A symphony of dark and light,
In harmony, our spirits rise.

With every heartbeat, echoes flow,
The universe in rhythmic grace.
In silence deep, our whispers grow,
Together, we embrace this space.

So let us wander, hand in hand,
In cosmic rhythms, beautifully.
As stars align across the land,
We find our place, eternally.

## Echoes of Oneness

In the stillness, we find our way,
Voices blend in a soft display.
Hearts intertwine, a shared embrace,
Together we dance in time and space.

Moments linger, whispers collide,
Unified spirits, nothing to hide.
In every heartbeat, we seek the truth,
A journey together, an ageless youth.

Through winds of change, we rise and soar,
Boundless horizons, forevermore.
Echoing laughter, a symphony bright,
In the shadow, we shine our light.

Like rivers merging, we flow as one,
Under the same stars, our story begun.
In the echoes, our souls align,
Woven together, our spirits entwine.

Embracing the silence, we hear the call,
In the fabric of being, we are all.
Cradled in unity, dreams take flight,
As echoes of oneness cradle the night.

# Infinite Synchronicity

In every heartbeat, a moment unfolds,
Patterns of life in stories retold.
Stars blink in rhythm, a cosmic dance,
Infinite synchronicity, a destined chance.

Waves of connection ripple through time,
Each little spark, a reason, a rhyme.
In silent whispers, we hear our fate,
Guided by forces both subtle and great.

Paths intertwine in the softest glow,
Life's perfect timing, so seamless, so flow.
In serendipity, our paths align,
Infinite threads in a tapestry divine.

Through the chaos, a calm prevails,
In the dance of existence, love never fails.
With trust in the journey, we learn to see,
The beauty of life in its harmony.

Every coincidence a sign to behold,
Life's grand design, a treasure untold.
As stars above offer their light,
In infinite synchronicity, dreams take flight.

## The Tapestry of Existence

Woven with colors both bold and bright,
Every thread tells a story of flight.
In the loom of life, we each play a part,
Creating the fabric that warms the heart.

From shadows to light, each journey unfolds,
In patterns and layers, our truth it holds.
A tapestry vast, with stories combined,
In the depths of connection, our spirits aligned.

Together we rise, with love as our guide,
In the dance of creation, we face the tide.
Every encounter, a stitch in the seam,
The tapestry grows, woven in dream.

In moments of silence, we hear the call,
The beauty of living, uniting us all.
In the grand design, we find our place,
In the tapestry of existence, we embrace.

With gratitude flowing, we cherish the weave,
In the threads of connection, we learn to believe.
Life's hopeful design, a masterpiece spun,
In the tapestry of existence, we are one.

# Threads of Shared Light

In the cosmos, sparks intertwine,
Illuminated paths where souls align.
Threads of shared light weave through the dark,
Creating a canvas, a vibrant arc.

In moments cherished, in laughter we share,
Together we flourish, a love so rare.
Through trials faced, our spirits unite,
In the warmth of connection, we ignite.

From hearts ablaze, a glow will emerge,
With each gentle touch, our spirits surge.
Through the shadows, we'll find our way,
In threads of shared light, we'll forever stay.

In the tapestry woven with joy and grace,
Each light a beacon, a sacred space.
In every heartbeat, in whispers of night,
We gather our courage, our threads shining bright.

Embracing the journey, in light we grow,
With every shared moment, love's essence we sow.
In the dance of existence, with hearts full and right,
We'll forever be bound by threads of shared light.

# Merging Currents of Being

In the quiet flow of dreams,
We drift like leaves in streams.
Embracing the light of day,
We learn to find our way.

Hands entwined in whispered hopes,
Together, we broaden our scopes.
The river carries us fast,
Binding future with the past.

In shadows where our spirits dance,
We find truth within each chance.
Waves of joy crash on our shore,
Each heartbeat echoes evermore.

Through storms that test our will,
Together, we climb each hill.
Merging currents, side by side,
In love, we always abide.

With every ebb and flow we share,
We learn to love, to truly care.
In this vast sea, we grow,
Merging currents, we'll always know.

# The Unseen Ties

In silence, we carve our path,
Unseen ties that bridge the gap.
Hearts whisper through the night,
Binding souls in soft daylight.

Through laughter and through tears,
We echo across the years.
Woven threads in fate's embrace,
In this dance, we find our place.

Moments shared in glances brief,
A tapestry of strength and grief.
Connected through the unseen arts,
We anchor each other's hearts.

Though distance may stretch wide and far,
Our ties shine like a guiding star.
In every heartbeat, love persists,
In unseen ways, we exist.

The bonds we share, a sacred song,
Where every note helps us belong.
Through life's maze, we walk aligned,
In unseen ties, our fate combined.

# Symphony of One Heart

In the stillness, chords align,
A symphony, your heart and mine.
Notes of longing fill the air,
In harmony, we find our care.

Each beat a measure, slow yet true,
Creating music just for two.
Resonating dreams in light,
Our melody takes flight.

Through joy and sorrow, crescendos rise,
In solace, love never dies.
Strings of fate, a perfect blend,
A song that never ends.

With every note, a story flows,
In rhythm, our love grows.
Symphony of souls entwined,
In every heartbeat, love defined.

Together, we compose our fate,
In this dance, we celebrate.
A symphony that sets us free,
In every chord, in you, in me.

# Constellation of Kindred Spirits

In the night, bright stars align,
Kindred souls in paths divine.
Across the vast celestial sea,
Our lights, forever meant to be.

Each sparkle shares a whispered tale,
A bond that time will never fail.
Woven through the cosmic dance,
In this space, we take our chance.

Through darkest hours, we shine bright,
Guiding each other with our light.
Constellations ever bold,
In unity, our stories unfold.

With gentle warmth, we intertwine,
In cosmic love, your heart is mine.
Together, we traverse the skies,
In kindred spirits, love never dies.

As the universe expands and shifts,
Our bond remains, a precious gift.
In this constellation's glow,
Together, we'll forever flow.

# Unyielding Ties

In shadows cast by days gone by,
We gather strength, you and I.
Together we'll face the testing storms,
In bond unbroken, love transforms.

With whispered dreams and silent vows,
We nurture roots beneath the boughs.
Through trials fierce, we stand as one,
An endless dance beneath the sun.

In laughter shared and sorrows too,
Each moment builds what we once knew.
A tapestry of lives entwined,
With every thread, our fates aligned.

Through winding paths that fate has cast,
Our hearts beat strong, our shadows last.
In the face of doubt, we choose to stay,
In every word, love finds its way.

So here we stand, forever bold,
In stories rich, together told.
Our unyielding ties shall never fray,
In every dawn, we find our way.

## The Pulse of Togetherness

Hearts entwined, a rhythmic beat,
In every glance, our souls repeat.
Together, we embrace the night,
In whispered dreams, we find our light.

Through laughter's grace, we dance along,
In every note, we craft our song.
With hands clasped tight, we journey far,
In unity, we are the star.

When shadows fall and dreams seem lost,
Together we will bear the cost.
With every challenge faced in stride,
We walk the path, with hope our guide.

In moments shared, we find our way,
Each heartbeat echoes what we say.
In harmony, our spirits rise,
In every tear, a new surprise.

So let us dance, our spirits soar,
In every bond, we're evermore.
With every breath, together known,
In this pulse of life, love has grown.

## Reflections of Unity

In mirrored smiles, our truths unfold,
A shared embrace that never grows old.
With gentle whispers in the night,
We forge our dreams in silver light.

Through trials faced and paths we tread,
In united strength, we move ahead.
Each laugh, a note in our refrain,
Together, we rise, through joy and pain.

In the dance of time, we intertwine,
With every heartbeat, your hand in mine.
In shadows cast by days of yore,
We find the courage to explore.

Each story told, a cherished thread,
In every word, our spirits fed.
With kindness offered, we find our grace,
Reflections of unity, our sacred space.

The echoes linger, soft and clear,
In every moment, I hold you near.
In every dawn, our hope restored,
Reflections of unity, forever adored.

# Harmonious Spirals

In spirals wide, our spirits twine,
A dance of colors, bright and fine.
Together we rise, a vibrant hue,
In this world, it's me and you.

With every step, we weave the thread,
In harmony, our joys widespread.
Through valleys low and mountains high,
We find our voice, we claim the sky.

With gentle hearts, we share the song,
In every note, we both belong.
In laughter's echo, in silence still,
Together, we find our shared will.

So let us spiral through the years,
With every joy and all our tears.
In this embrace, we learn and grow,
Harmonious spirals, together flow.

And as we journey, hand in hand,
In this melody, we take a stand.
With love as our guide, we dance as one,
In these harmonious spirals, we've just begun.

# A Dance of Interwoven Fates

In shadows where the whispers play,
Two souls meet in a timeless sway.
Their paths entwined like vines of night,
Each step a spark, each glance a light.

With rhythm born from heartbeats shared,
They dance as if the world has cared.
Through storms and calm, through joy and ache,
In every turn, their bond won't break.

In silent vows, their spirits soar,
The echoes of their love explore.
A tapestry of laughter spun,
In fate's embrace, they both are one.

With every twirl, the cosmos sighs,
As moonlight bathes their tender ties.
In every breath, a promise made,
Their dance will last, never to fade.

Through twilight hues, their journey gleams,
A union formed from intertwined dreams.
As stars align, their hearts will find,
In every beat, they're gently blind.

## The Infinite Embrace

In the stillness of the night,
Two hearts convene, a longing flight.
With every sigh, their souls entwine,
An endless realm, a space divine.

Time may slip like grains of sand,
In this embrace, they understand.
A universe contained within,
Their love, a place where dreams begin.

Each whisper stirs the cosmic air,
A symphony beyond compare.
As galaxies sway in tender grace,
They find their truth in the vast space.

In every touch, a spark ignites,
Illuminating shadowed nights.
With open hearts, they dive beneath,
To grasp the essence of their wreath.

Together on this sacred path,
They seek the infinite, the aftermath.
In timeless dance, they share the glow,
In every breath, their spirits flow.

# Interconnected Dreams

Beneath the veil of sleeping skies,
Awake the dreams that softly rise.
In realms where thoughts and wishes blend,
Each moment shared, they transcend.

With every heartbeat, visions flow,
A tapestry of hopes in tow.
The threads of fate begin to weave,
In this connection, they believe.

In starlit fields where wishes roam,
Their spirits dance, a sacred home.
Each heartbeat echoes, loud and clear,
In every dream, the other near.

From whispered secrets to shimmering light,
They wander through the endless night.
With open minds and hearts so free,
In interconnected harmony.

As dawn awakens, shadows wane,
Their dreams remain, a sweet refrain.
Through silent whispers, still they see,
In every dream, they'll always be.

## Reflections in the Collective

Among the tides of thoughts that flow,
A mirror holds the truths we know.
In every face, a story found,
In whispers soft, the echoes sound.

The bonds we share in silent grace,
In every glance, a warm embrace.
Our hopes reflected, spirits blend,
In this collective, hearts transcend.

Each voice a note in the grand refrain,
Together singing joy and pain.
In fragile moments, strength arises,
In shared connections, love comprises.

With every tear, a lesson learned,
In unity, the souls have yearned.
As shadows shift and colors change,
In reflection, lives interchange.

So let us weave this vibrant art,
In every inch, we play a part.
As one, we rise, together thrive,
In reflections deep, we're truly alive.

# Strands of Everlasting Light

In the dusk of fading day,
Whispers dance in gentle sway,
Threads of hope, a soft embrace,
Guiding souls through time and space.

Stars ignite the endless night,
Casting beams of purest light,
Woven hearts in silver seams,
Together crafting vibrant dreams.

Across the vast and silent sky,
With every breath, we learn to fly,
Embers glow in twilight's kiss,
Chasing shadows, finding bliss.

Through the storms and raging seas,
We hold tight to memories,
In each heart, a luminous spark,
Lighting paths within the dark.

As dawn unveils its golden hue,
The world awakens, fresh and new,
Each strand gleams with love's own light,
Forever shining, pure and bright.

# Navigating the Sea of Souls

In the depths where echoes roam,
Waves of whispers call us home,
Vessels sail on tides of fate,
Seeking bonds that never wait.

Currents pull with gentle might,
Guiding dreams through tranquil night,
Stars above, they chart our course,
Bearing hearts with endless force.

Each ripple holds a story shared,
Of battles fought and love declared,
Through storms that test our very core,
We find the strength to seek and soar.

As shores emerge with life anew,
We navigate with hearts so true,
In every wave, a tale unfolds,
Uniting souls, their journeys bold.

Together on this endless sea,
We sail on, forever free,
Finding light in unity,
Navigating endlessly.

# The Fabric of Existence

Threads of time intertwined tight,
Woven patterns in the night,
Every moment, every breath,
Stitching life through love and death.

Colors blend in sacred art,
Each strand beats like a tender heart,
In the tapestry of dreams,
Life is more than what it seems.

Every laugh, and every tear,
Holds a whisper, crystal clear,
Fractals of our shared embrace,
Crafting beauty in this space.

With hands that weave the tales of old,
We share the warmth through stories told,
Each knot a bond, each thread a hope,
In this fabric, we learn to cope.

Beneath the stars, our spirits sing,
Entwined together, hope takes wing,
The fabric of existence glows,
In each heart, a love that grows.

# Threads of Harmony

In the hush of twilight's grace,
Melodies find their gentle place,
Every note, a heartbeat's quest,
Threads of harmony expressed.

From the whispers of the breeze,
To the rustle of the trees,
Nature sings both soft and bright,
Binding all in pure delight.

Voices blend in sweet refrain,
In the joy, we feel no pain,
Holding close the dreams we weave,
In each other, we believe.

Through the seasons, life will sway,
In its dance, we find our way,
Colors merge in sunset's hue,
Every thread connects me to you.

In this space, where souls align,
We are woven, you and I,
Threads of harmony, our song,
Together is where we belong.

# Cosmic Continuum

In the expanse where stars ignite,
Galaxies swirl in endless flight.
Planets hum a cosmic tune,
Beneath the watchful silver moon.

Time stretches like a vibrant thread,
Woven stories of dreams once spread.
Matter dances with light's embrace,
Infinite wonders in boundless space.

Stardust whispers of ancient lore,
Echoes linger from yonder shore.
Each heartbeat in this vast night,
Reflects the universe's light.

As comets carve their fleeting paths,
We marvel at the cosmic baths.
Eons blend in a spiral swirl,
A tapestry of the cosmic pearl.

In this realm of dark and bright,
Every shadow births a light.
We are part of this grand design,
Eternal echoes in space align.

# Bridges Across Time

Time's river flows, a silent stream,
Each moment caught in a woven dream.
Bridges rise from heart to heart,
Connecting souls though worlds apart.

In laughter shared, in tears we find,
Threads of life intricately twined.
Footprints linger on paths once tread,
Whispers of love that never fled.

Across the ages, voices call,
Through winding corridors, we stand tall.
With every story, every rhyme,
We build our bridges across time.

Seasons change, yet bonds remain,
Joy and sorrow, love and pain.
In the tapestry of the divine,
We stitch our hopes and dreams in line.

Together we wander, hearts aligned,
In past and future, forever intertwined.
Time's embrace holds us ever tight,
In this journey from dark to light.

# The Essence of Us

In a world painted with gentle hues,
We find the essence of me and you.
Threads of kindness weave our fate,
In silent love, we resonate.

Moments flicker like stars that shine,
In tender glances, our hearts entwine.
With every laugh and every sigh,
We etch our truth in the endless sky.

Time, a canvas, our lives reside,
Colors merging, side by side.
Through gentle storms and sunny days,
We explore life's wondrous ways.

In whispered dreams and soft goodbyes,
Our essence mirrors the starlit skies.
With every heartbeat, our spirits soar,
An endless journey to explore.

Together we dance in this timeless ballet,
Crafting memories that never fray.
In the essence of us, we find our grace,
Two souls united in a sacred space.

## Celestial Kinship

In the realm where stardust flows,
A bond unites all that knows.
Celestial kinship calls us near,
In cosmic whispers, crystal clear.

Galaxies twirl in a cosmic embrace,
Painting the night with beauty and grace.
Within the heart of the night sky,
We find the reason, the where and why.

Glimmers of fate in the universe spin,
Each life's journey, where we begin.
From the depths of darkness, light is born,
A testament to the love we've worn.

Together we weave a tapestry bright,
Each thread connecting in heavenly light.
As stars align, we share the dream,
In our hearts, a celestial gleam.

In timeless moments, we rise and soar,
Through cosmic realms, we are evermore.
For in this journey, hand in hand,
We discover kinship across the land.

# Eternal Threads of Connection

In shadows cast by fleeting light,
We weave our dreams through endless night.
Each heartbeat sings a silent song,
Binding us where we belong.

Through joys and sorrows, hand in hand,
Together we will always stand.
With every tear and every laugh,
We stitch our fate, a woven path.

Like rivers flow through ancient lands,
Our souls entwined, a fate that spans.
In every glance, in every touch,
We find the love that means so much.

Across the stars, in cosmic dance,
We find the strength in every chance.
Each moment shared, a thread divine,
In this grand tapestry, we shine.

Eternal connections, strong and true,
Through time and space, I'll reach for you.
Together we create a spark,
Illuminating every dark.

# Tapestry of Souls

In colors bright, our stories blend,
Each thread a journey, every bend.
With every knot, we tie our fates,
In this grand weave, love narrates.

The fabric stretches, never tears,
Through winds of change, it always dares.
Embroidered patterns, rich and bold,
A testament of life retold.

Together we stand, a vibrant hue,
In shades of passion, pure and true.
United by dreams we dare to share,
A tapestry beyond compare.

Whispers of past in every seam,
Woven with hope, stitched with a dream.
A dance of souls in twilight's glow,
In every thread, our love will flow.

Through life's great loom, we forge our way,
In dusk's embrace and dawn's first ray.
With every weave, our spirits soar,
In this tapestry, forevermore.

# Whispers Beyond Time

In the silence, secrets dwell,
Echoes of thoughts, more than we tell.
Through ages past, they softly speak,
In timeless realms, we seek the peak.

The stars align to share their grace,
In whispers soft, they find their place.
Through murmurs of the moonlit night,
We grasp the threads of purest light.

In gardens where the shadows play,
Every whisper guides our way.
A tapestry woven with care,
Connecting hearts both near and rare.

Moments fleeting like autumn leaves,
Each whisper tells of what it believes.
From ages past to futures wide,
In whispered dreams, we shall abide.

Beyond the veil, our voices blend,
With open hearts, we will transcend.
Through whispers sweet, we are made whole,
Binding the essence of each soul.

## Harmony in the Cosmos

In the cosmos, stars align,
Each heartbeat resonates, divine.
Planets dance in orbits vast,
A symphony of shadows cast.

The universe sings, a timeless tune,
In harmony under the watchful moon.
Galaxies swirl in endless chase,
Every moment holds a trace.

Through constellations, stories weave,
In gentle whispers, we believe.
Each note a echo of love's refrain,
In cosmic chords, we feel no pain.

The sun and moon, in rhythm sway,
Breathing life into each day.
In every star, our hopes ignite,
Creating magic in the night.

Together we rise, like light on sea,
In the cosmos, just you and me.
In endless harmony, we'll soar,
Boundless love forevermore.

# Merging Horizons

Beneath the glowing twilight sky,
Two worlds meet as colors blend.
The light of dreams begins to fly,
As day and night become a friend.

Glimmers trace the edge of dawn,
Whispers in the cooling air.
With each heartbeat, hope is drawn,
In the silence, love lays bare.

Mountains rise, the valleys sigh,
Time stands still in radiant grace.
The stars above begin to cry,
For in this moment, we embrace.

With every step, we weave the thread,
Of fate that binds our restless hearts.
Our dreams take flight, like birds we've fed,
As twilight's promise gently starts.

In a dance of shadows, we unite,
Embracing what the future holds.
Together in this fleeting light,
We find our story yet unfolds.

# The Dance of Souls


In the quiet of a midnight hour,
Two souls meet beneath the stars.
A spark ignites, a gentle power,
Their rhythms clash, like distant cars.

Each movement flows like flowing streams,
A choreography of the heart.
In every glance, a world of dreams,
Together, never far apart.

The music swells beyond the night,
Two hearts in tune, a perfect beat.
In every turn, they find their light,
As echoes of the past retreat.

With each embrace, the universe bends,
In the circle of love's warm glow.
This dance continues; it never ends,
A timeless journey that we know.

As stars align in their sweet flight,
A testament to love's great call.
In the darkness, they shine bright,
For together, they can conquer all.

## Limitless Connection

In the vastness, hearts collide,
With whispers shared on cosmic winds.
A bond unbroken, side by side,
As time and space begin to blend.

Every thought, a thread that weaves,
A tapestry of dreams untold.
In this realm, where nothing leaves,
Their stories are forever bold.

The heart speaks loud beyond the stars,
Where distance fades and skies align.
In silent echoes, love leaves scars,
Transforming darkness into shine.

Invisible ties connect their souls,
Bridging the gaps of night and day.
In this world, they play their roles,
As twilight turns to dawn's soft sway.

Limitless in every sense,
Their laughter dances through the night.
In unity, they find defense,
For together, they are the light.

## Interstellar Bonds

Between the stars, our spirits soar,
As galaxies begin to spin.
A dance of light forevermore,
A symphony where love begins.

From planet's edge to cosmic shore,
Our hearts connect—undefined space.
In this void, we find much more,
A universe of warm embrace.

Each pulse and beat, a journey drawn,
Through nebulas and starlit skies.
Together we will greet the dawn,
No boundaries where our essence lies.

In the quiet, we hear the song,
Of cosmic waves that guide our way.
In the silence, we both belong,
In this vastness, come what may.

Interstellar bonds, forever cast,
In the fabric of time, we thrive.
In love's embrace, we are steadfast,
As one, we dance, forever alive.

# Strength in Diversity

In colors bright, we stand together,
Each thread unique, woven like leather.
Through differences, our voices rise,
In unity, we find the prize.

Cultures blend, like rivers flow,
In harmony, we let love grow.
Embrace the varied, learn their ways,
In shared hearts, the hope displays.

From each story, wisdom shines,
In scattered seeds, a garden twines.
With open minds, we break the mold,
A tapestry of strength to hold.

Together we dance, a vibrant show,
Through laughter and tears, our spirits glow.
In strength we rise, hand in hand,
A chorus of voices, forever grand.

Each soul a note in a grand refrain,
In diversity, we find our gain.
Celebrate the difference, let it be,
In every heartbeat, true harmony.

# Unseen Connections

Beneath the surface, currents flow,
Silent whispers, we may not know.
Threads of fate weave us tight,
In darkness too, we find the light.

Eyes may wander, hearts may roam,
Yet in silence, we feel at home.
Invisible ties pull us close,
In quiet moments, love will grow.

When paths align, sparks ignite,
In simple smiles, shared delight.
Across the miles, a heartbeat thrums,
In each farewell, a teardrop hums.

No distance can sever what's intertwined,
In every story, our souls are aligned.
A network forged from joy and strife,
In unseen ways, we connect to life.

In shadows cast, we find our way,
Through empathy, we learn to stay.
With open hearts, we bridge the gaps,
In unseen threads, the world unmaps.

# The Strains of Together

In gentle hands, we hold the weight,
The strains of life, we navigate.
Through trials faced, we share the load,
In every heart, a love bestowed.

When storms arise, we find our place,
In unity, we embrace the grace.
Each burden shared, a lighter path,
In joyful moments, we escape the wrath.

Together we laugh, together we cry,
In every whisper, love does not die.
Through winding roads, we learn to bend,
In every turn, our spirits mend.

With every note, our song combines,
Through every challenge, our strength defines.
In togetherness, resilience grows,
The bonds we forge, like rivers flow.

Though seasons change, our roots run deep,
In connected hearts, our dreams we keep.
Through every strain, our voices blend,
In the dance of life, we find our trend.

# Resonance of Life

In softest whispers, nature sings,
The resonance of life, it brings.
From mountain peaks to ocean's roar,
In every heartbeat, we explore.

The wind tells tales of days gone by,
In rustling leaves, we hear the sigh.
Each petal falls, a gentle kiss,
In fleeting moments, we find bliss.

The stars above, they weave our dreams,
In twilight's glow, the hope redeems.
Through moonlit nights, our souls take flight,
In darkness deep, we find our light.

A rhythm flows in every breath,
In life's embrace, we conquer death.
Each pulse, a story, waiting to rise,
In echoes shared, our spirits fly.

In laughter's chord, our hearts align,
In sorrow's strain, our strength defines.
Through every song, the essence of we,
In life's resonance, we come to be.

# The Harmony of Echoes

In the valley where whispers play,
Soft notes of nature float and sway.
Each sound a story, old yet bright,
Carried on the wings of night.

The trees hum low, the rivers sigh,
As stars peek down from the sky.
In every echo, a tale unfurls,
Uniting hearts in a dance of swirls.

The mountains hold secrets deep and vast,
Guarding the songs from the past.
Time bends gently in this serene space,
A tapestry woven with grace.

Soft melodies drift on the breeze,
Filling the air with tranquil ease.
In this harmony, all souls align,
Creating a world so divine.

Underneath the moon's gentle glow,
The echoes of love begin to grow.
In this symphony of heartbeats near,
Life's sweetest music is always clear.

## Beyond Boundaries

Across the hills where dreams do soar,
Lies a world waiting, longing for more.
Through the clouds and over the sea,
Endless horizons call to you and me.

Paths unwritten, footsteps untread,
Adventures await, and fears we shed.
With every leap, we break the mold,
Daring the unknown, brave and bold.

The sun sets low, painting the sky,
Colors igniting, spirits fly high.
In the stillness, moments expand,
Uniting our hearts, hand in hand.

Together we wander, far and wide,
With hope in our hearts as our guide.
For in every journey, we find our way,
Beyond boundaries, come what may.

Whispers of courage echo inside,
Embracing the fears that once tried.
With trust in our steps, we dare to roam,
For beyond the limits, we find our home.

# Intertwined Journeys

Two paths that meet in the soft twilight,
A serendipitous moment, pure delight.
Hands connect, weaving stories anew,
In the dance of life, just me and you.

The road may twist and often turn,
Yet in each challenge, our spirits learn.
Together we step, through shadows and light,
Creating memories that shine so bright.

Each adventure, a chapter penned,
With laughter and love that shall never end.
Through valleys deep and mountains high,
We forge our bond as the stars reply.

With every heartbeat, we share, we grow,
In the tapestry of life, our threads flow.
Entwined forever, through thick and thin,
A journey enriched by the love within.

Through storms we wander, yet remain strong,
In this journey, together we belong.
With footsteps in sync and dreams aligned,
Intertwined journeys, a love defined.

# The Web of Life

Threads of silver, woven tight,
Connecting all in the morning light.
In every strand, a tale to tell,
Of joy and sorrow, where spirits dwell.

The dance of trees, the laughter of streams,
Each heartbeat echoes our shared dreams.
In the fabric of being, we find our place,
In the web of life, a graceful embrace.

Through loss and gain, we learn to bend,
With each connection, we begin to mend.
Hands reaching out, across the divide,
In unity's strength, we take pride.

The stars above shine down so bright,
Guiding our journeys through the night.
In every moment, we find our way,
In this web of life, love's grand display.

Together we build, through laughter and tears,
A legacy woven through all our years.
In the heart of existence, we find our strife,
Celebrating each thread in the web of life.